Becoming a Fish

by Grace Hansen

Abdo
CHANGING ANIMALS
Kids

Abdo Kids Jumbo is an Imprint of Abdo Kids
abdopublishing.com

abdopublishing.com

Published by Abdo Kids, a division of ABDO, P.O. Box 398166, Minneapolis, Minnesota 55439.
Copyright © 2019 by Abdo Consulting Group, Inc. International copyrights reserved in all countries.
No part of this book may be reproduced in any form without written permission from the publisher.
Abdo Kids Jumbo™ is a trademark and logo of Abdo Kids.

052018

092018

Photo Credits: Alamy, iStock, Shutterstock

Production Contributors: Teddy Borth, Jennie Forsberg, Grace Hansen

Design Contributors: Dorothy Toth, Laura Mitchell

Library of Congress Control Number: 2017960558

Publisher's Cataloging-in-Publication Data

Names: Hansen, Grace, author.

Title: Becoming a fish / by Grace Hansen.

Description: Minneapolis, Minnesota : Abdo Kids, 2019. | Series: Changing animals |
    Includes glossary, index and online resources (page 24).

Identifiers: ISBN 9781532108150 (lib.bdg.) | ISBN 9781532109133 (ebook) |
    ISBN 9781532109621 (Read-to-me ebook)

Subjects: LCSH: Fishes--Juvenile literature. | Animal life cycles--Juvenile literature. |
    Metamorphosis--Juvenile literature. | Animal behavior--Juvenile literature.

Classification: DDC 571.876--dc23

Table of Contents

Stage 1

Many fish grow and change
in similar ways. All fish begin
as eggs.

Northern pike lay their eggs in calm, shallow waters that have lots of plants. They lay a few eggs at a time.

6

7

Eggs are sticky and yellowish in color. The eggs attach to the plants.

9

Stage 2

After about 10 days, an egg hatches. The newly hatched pike eats **yolk** from its own egg. It grows a bit stronger. Soon it is ready to swim.

11

Stage 3

The young pike is now called a **fry**. It swims freely. It no longer relies on its egg **yolk** for food. It can now eat **zooplankton** and tiny insect eggs.

Stage 4

The **fry** eats and grows. It

grows scales and working fins.

It is called a **fingerling** now.

Fingerlings grow very fast!

Stage 5

Soon, the **fingerling** looks more like an adult fish. It catches and eats larger meals, like other fish.

16

Stage 6

A full-grown pike is an adult. It lies still in areas filled with plants. It waits for food to swim by. It loves to eat!

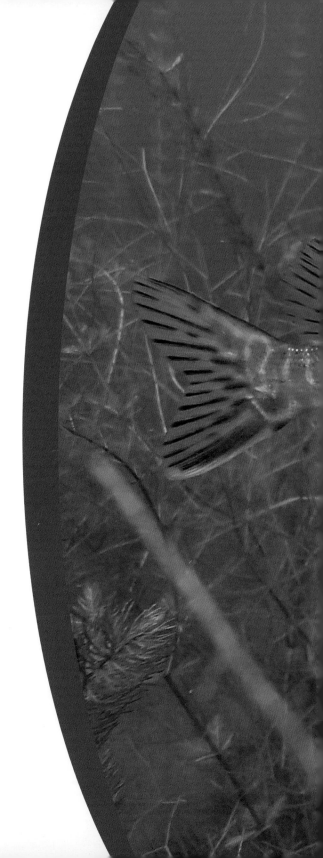

Stage 7

After around 3 to 5 years,
northern pike are ready to
spawn. Females lay their eggs.
And the cycle begins again!

20

More Facts

- A salmon's life cycle is very complex compared to other fish's.

- Eggs laid in warm water hatch faster than eggs laid in cold water.

- Most eggs do not survive. Changing water temperature and oxygen levels, floods, and being eaten by other animals are some reasons eggs do not hatch.

Glossary

fingerling – a young fish that has grown scales and has working fins.

fry – a very small and very young fish that has grown to a point where it can feed itself.

spawn – to produce a large number of eggs.

yolk – the part of an egg that is rich in nutrients.

zooplankton – tiny animals that drift in oceans, seas, and bodies of fresh water.

Index

Abdo Kids
ONLINE

FREE! ONLINE MULTIMEDIA RESOURCES

Visit abdokids.com and use this code to access crafts, games, videos, and more!

Abdo Kids Code:
CBK8150